Of the Heart & Of the Soul.

Every Journey in life

has a beginning...

Charlie Hirst

ISBN: 9798822067127

DEDICATION.

This book is dedicated to Sheila Porter.

Thank you for lighting that spark all those years ago and showing me that I could do anything and be anything I wanted.

And to Ale, who reconnected me with who I am.

CONTENTS.

FOREWORD.

Charlie has described the beauties and pains of life in such poetic ways within this incredible read, which comes as no surprise having known Charlie for many years.

Throughout his lifetime he has always very naturally been able to enlighten others through his powerful words of wisdom and I have personally learned through him that without standing tall in our authenticity and expressing our truth, we rob ourselves of the lives we so desire and dream.

This collection of poetic pages has been so beautifully created. Written between the ages of sixteen to twenty-one, Charlie took the time to explore his life's experiences and emotions, whilst illustrating his revelations and uncovering the start of his self-discovery journey through the power of poetry.

His warm, loving and empathetic heart shines through each piece. Each one uncovering a new emotion, whilst guiding you to go within and discover more of self. This truly is poetry that enlightens as well as sings.

Describing all the realms of mind, body and soul through expression in such magical ways – I couldn't recommend this read more. And knowing him as the extraordinary, caring and genuine individual that he is, I know that every word has come from the depths of his heart and soul.

Charlie is someone who has experienced, overcome and accomplished much within his lifetime; and through his experiences has not only learned more about life itself, he has also now truly been able to step into his power and share his discoveries with others through the power of illuminating speech and literature.

His award-winning communication skillsets are now being shared with the world and are gifting others who read or listen to him a wonderful experience of educational and poetic enlightenment.

Ale Ramirez
Life Coach and founder of Your Growth Game.

INTRODUCTION.

When I was much younger, I started my journey in life with a carefree, happy-go-lucky attitude and no plan. As I grew, things happened and I had no idea how to cope, but I am not unique in this. We all start out in life with no idea where we are going to end up or how we are going to get to wherever it is! We all set out blindly believing that on some level everything will turn out O.K. and we will somehow leave a legacy for those who follow us.

Some drift along, some find their purpose early, and some never find it. The problem is that no matter who you are, or what you decide to do, there is no definitive instruction manual on how to get the best out of life. No guide to show us ways past the pitfalls, hurdles or even how to deal with the successes. Sure, we can listen to friends and family, but they are not walking our path, so what worked for them might not work for us.

Between the ages of sixteen and about twenty-one, I wrote down how I felt; my pain, anguish, frustrations, realizations and the truths I knew at that time. Looking back, some of the language and understanding I had, now seems childlike and innocent, but that's the point of life – we all change and grow whether we choose to or not. At the time of writing these poems, the words, the feelings and the truths were real and authentic. Little did I know how my life would evolve and change over the next thirty years!

Even though I have grown, changed, learnt, understood and evolved since those days, and I continuously try to be more than I was yesterday, I am grateful that I took the time to write down how I felt all those years ago, as it serves as a reminder how far I have come. Re-reading these poems I have come to understand that they still have great relevance to my journey to date and there are still lessons that I need to learn.

Every journey begins somewhere. We all have our own individual starting points, our unique journey to make, and our own dreams to follow. But we all have one thing in common – we all started at our own beginning and life will throw us curveballs or 'plot-twists' and we have to figure out how to overcome them. My hope is that these poems can serve as an illustration of no matter how dark things seem at the time, there will always be a way to surmount the issues life throws our way.

Every journey has a beginning, and this was mine….

Charlie

Castle.

Again, I sit in caverns old,
Above the rugged, barren cliff top.
Beneath, the waves that pound for entry
To ruined secrets, and life within.
I sit and watch the rolling sea
From a 'war-like' wound within the wall:
A gateway for remembered glances,
And tears shed for a distant soul.

The ceaseless waves pound eternal –
A heartbeat for the memory.
I see you sit so close beside me;
With tranquil, radiant, peaceful smile.
And through the tearful, blurred emotion
You take my hand and hold me fast,
To tell me that I'm not alone,
The light came back to a haunted past.

There is no time within these stones,
Where I call you here to sit beside me.
A simple infinite lasting kiss
As waves barrage the rocks below.
And gulls cry out, from far above
lonely, piercing yet hopeful notes
and the blinding sun, so iridescent
of things that were, will be, who knows?

CELESTIAL DANCE.

I am the Sun around your Moon
Our child, the Earth, around we watch
Giving both light and love.
I am the Consort as you are the Queen
Our love is the balanced circle –
A dance by which we weave.
Yours is the silver as mine is the gold;
Apart, alone, and pure in essence.
Together a myriad of rainbows.
Together as one, high on the tree
Seeing around the cosmos unfold,
Time in an instant.

SOCIABLY CONFUSED.

The blind vision of square circles,
A loving hatred in bright darkness,
Simply difficult.

The perfect imperfection of the living dead,
A foolish wise man in dry water,
Sociably confused.

Subordinate superiority in high powered inertia,
The literary illiterate are blind seers,
Organized chaos.

The blissful terror of clear confusion,
The conformist rebel a wealthy pauper,
Mad sanity.

MONOLITH.

Beneath the moon on fields of green, between the valley sides
A crumbled moss-grown monolith shows where my one love lies.
She is bold and truly beautiful, but holds a heart of stone;
The single time I held her glance, she chilled me to the bone.

Once a year I visit her, but all year long I wait,
I sit and think of what may be and hurl abuse at fate.
I wait and listen to the waning beat of distant drums,
To signify that very soon my one true love will come.

A chill descends and wraps the air with tendrils of grey haar,
Approaching whispers on the wings of angels from afar.
And there she stands, a perfect dream, cloaked in lights of grey;
No glance towards my shredded soul, before she moves away.

Next year, again, I will return and hope that she has changed:
To come with me and live once more in lands from whence I came.
I long to see my native home, and rest within its peace,
But vow to stay beside my love, until all time has ceased.

BLUSHING SMILER.

Many times, and many thoughts
And half a year gone by.
So how do you invade my dreams?
I've still no reason as to why.

We'd sat and talked through topics,
But never to the point.
Dragged my feet when I'd come close
To saying what I really want.

My little blushing smiler,
Who warms my heart throughout.
You're here and give an inner peace:
But all my dreams are plagued with doubt.

The mystery that shrouds you
Draws me in and turns me round:
A storm-tossed cork upon the sea
With feet that never touch the ground.

But still we sit, and still we talk
For hours upon hours.
How can one so old and young
Transfix me with a wistful smile?

Courage I'll just have to pluck
From some deep place within
So then, in time, I'll make my point
And see me doubt free dream begin.

PHOENIX.

Standing like roses,
Thorns in the wind,
My keen points insignificant
At piercing her skin.
The light that surrounds her,
The spark from her eyes;
I'm a pointless survivor
From a war deep inside.
But riding forever
On the wings of a storm,
The crashing and burning
Will not be forlorn.
For out of the fire,
From the flames and the heat
One phoenix emerges,
Whole and complete.

REGRETS.

I

I regret I never said goodbye
The day I left your shore.
But the one thing I can't handle,
Is seeing you no more.
They say that parting is sweet sorrow,
But I cannot really say,
Because I never truly met you
In our time up to today.

But I can say I've watched you,
Albeit from afar;
Your eyes I do remember
Were smoking pools of fire.
They purveyed temptation just so far
To a place I never reached.
Sirocco eyes invade my dreams
To the point I cannot sleep.

Your smile it seems was made in heaven,
So perfect and serene.
It calls my soul from hidden depths,
To bridge the gaps between.
Your laugh, I feel, could call up wonders
From far off foreign lands.
I know I'm called back to you
To fill those empty arms.

Your soul does not belong down here
But flying upon wings.
With perfect grace, a love embrace,
To make the godhead sing.
All other beings pale beside
Your breathless, timeless beauty.
I wonder if I'll have the chance
To know you, love you truly.

II

Remember Rod who sang the song
Of sailing stormy waters?
I have now come to calmer seas,
My steps have never faltered.

Remember when I sang this song
Into your misty eyes?
The pain and joy which we both felt
Made dreams I have alive.

Remember when you held me close
And filled these empty arms?
And with our lips in tight embrace,
My soul and body sang.

Remember, love, the day I left
And never said goodbye?
I shall now never leave your side
Until the day I die.

IS THIS IT?

From the moment that I met you
My life and world turned upside down.
The tranquil peace I always felt
On days I knew you were around.
I admit I often stole a glance
Just to see you from afar;
Your face, your smile, your eyes, your lips;
But to let you know, I'd never dare.

"Is this it?" I'd often wonder,
As you maybe looked my way.
I could never grasp my full felt courage
And ask if, perhaps, you felt the same.
I realise I've missed many chances
As days and nights have passed me by,
To know the maybe fatal truth
And finding out the reasons why.

But still I always ask myself
Those three deep and mystic words
Whose answer will solve all my doubts
Of how I feel. But it's absurd,
I sit and write these silly lines
Right now, I know you'll never see.
I'm caught in traps, my own soul's making
And I've not the courage to speak for real.

So here I'll sit, remain to wonder,
If what I feel is returned in kind.
But just maybe in conversation
I'll say what's really on my mind.
Until then we'll remain the same
Not knowing what each other thinks.
My hope is there, but then again
Who knows what fortune tomorrow brings?

THE SULK.

I'll never love,
I know that now,
In memories I'll grow.
But with what you gave,
My life is saved,
Although my soul is gone.

I'll just sit here,
And in my mind
Your images I'll see.
Smiling, laughing,
Sirocco eyes,
That now don't look at me.

But as is said,
Life does go on.
Advice I think is best.
Though deep inside,
I know they'll find
A hole inside my chest.

SEASONS.

I measure life in many ways
Of things I've seen and done.
Cherished memories held so close,
Beneath a winter's sun.

A lingered glance that meant so much,
I read the thoughts too soon.
A laugh, a smile, a treasured touch,
Beneath the summer moon.

An evening of exquisite taste,
Out with the sight of walls.
Forever gliding onwards, towards
Autumn's coloured halls.

And now, my love, how do you feel
With all that has been done.
Do you wish, or think of things
That once we did in fun?

YOUR CALL.

I remember, years ago, feelings such as these
Within, my heart and soul upturned
Unable to find peace.
Every time I close my eyes to gather in my thoughts
Sirocco eyes will shyly smile,
And focus turns to naught.

The prospect of not seeing you fills me with such a fear:
But thoughts of you, a slow deep breath,
I smile from ear to ear.
I have much I wish to say, but fear to speak too soon;
If I do, you may reject –
I'll howl it to the moon.

I want to see you daily; the long and sleepless nights
To talk, and share my inner soul
Which I know that I've held tight.
But for now, I'll settle for an aspect of your heart
And thus, the ball is in your court,
Your call, my love, you start.

GONE.

He loved her more than he dare say
From memories he held so close.
Thrice ten months since he last held her
When heat and passion then arose.

Her hair was blonde, her eyes deep brown.
Alluring smiles to greet his day.
Her sunny laugh prolonged for hours
As through the world she made her way.

Through all long days and longer nights
The love between them deepened still.
And those that knew them joked around,
With words that boded good, not ill.

Yet more than that, they were true friends –
Their hopes and fears did they expound.
No memories were left unaired
And soon their love was real, profound.

But days went past, and time flew by,
He felt inside a hopelessness.
Taken from him was she to be,
But never could he love her less.

And on one cold December day
She took a trip to get back home.
Their parting tears were bittersweet –
Both knew inside their time was done.

Even though he could not hold her,
A parting promise again to meet.
'Twas just the thought of when and where,
Then as before, whole, complete.

Then news arrived, her plane had crashed,
And all bar none were left for dead.
He howled in rage, he laughed, he cried.
His world destroyed; his love betrayed.

He loved her more than he dare say,
The memories are all he has.
Now he lives to walk beside her –
In dreams and thoughts, she's back at last.

HINDSIGHT.

As the winds of time whispered
Across the endless desert.
The howling banshees screeched
A warning of impending doom.
As she sat in her rocker
On the porch of possibilities.
She cried out, vainly warning,
Not to make the same mistakes.

The winds of time grew fresh
Around his battered, worn out feet.
He thought he caught a far-off whisper
Of voices raised in desperation.
The winds of time around him howled;
To scar his emotion, drive him insane.
He realised what was being said,
Not to make the same mistakes again.

He stopped and stood; reality dawned –
He was in the steps of previous journeys.
He looked round with hind-sights glasses
People, places, friendships, Her.
The truth of what was being said
Raised its way to understanding.
He couldn't risk to lose this chance,
Of making good, to end pretending.

He turned around, retraced his steps
Back along the windblown sands.
Called forth the courage of yesteryear,
Walked back for miles to hold her hand.
He told her of an old grey woman
And of the warning cries of winds,
He told her then and there he loved her
And wouldn't make mistakes again.

CAN'T REMEMBER.

I can't remember when I felt,
On days and nights like these.
Where we sat and caught a glance
Into each other's misty eyes.

I can't remember the way I felt
The way I do out here.
Endless chances, unsaid thoughts,
Which open up our fears.

I'll never tell the way I feel
Even when you look my way:
But I'll just sit here in painful silence,
Until my dying day.

FIRST DATE.

Anxious moments crawled along
As he sat amidst his fears.
Nervous glance towards an ancient timepiece,
As he hoped that she'd appear.

Those around just seemed to watch
As he waited, glass in hand.
He knew the fashion of being late,
And hoped that was her plan.

Without warning, in she glided,
Nervous smiles as she took her seat.
He now understood, her fears were greater
As both began to drink and eat.

The conversation stumbled,
Rocked its way, till both relaxed.
Un-joined streams of topics wandered,
Friendship grew from where they sat.

As he sipped a beer he watched,
Listened, by the gas firelight.
His fear reduced; emotions heightened.
Now, no doubt, that this was right.

Then to meet the family man,
To reassure his child was sound.
The relaxed atmosphere continued.
Time now for a final round.

As they went their separate ways,
Knowing much remained unsaid.
They said they'd meet tomorrow night
To find out where this new path led.

SHOULD I?

Should I go back and ask her
If it's me she really craves?
To hold her in the lonely nights
'till sun begins a brand-new day.

Should I wait a day and see
If things progress as I've planned?
The joining of two single souls
As one beneath the heavens span.

Should I just give up the ghost,
Just turn and walk away?
Thus, never know if what I felt,
Was felt by her on any day.

Or will she come towards me,
And tell me how she feels?
Initiate a love embrace
And hold me so I know it's real.

MIRRORS.

In the heat of the night
Surrounding peace is cold.
Just mirrored reflections
Within, without my soul.

A coloured TV screen,
Displayed for all to see.
And mirrored reflections,
On show eternally.

A non-sense fight, cross words,
Said in the peak of day.
Show mirrored reflections
Shatter - fade away.

A soft and gentle touch
External to the core.
A mirrored reflection,
Invited through the door.

A whispered web-like kiss
Floats through the air to heart.
And mirrored reflections
Rebound it back in part.

UTOPIAN DREAMS.

In a dream of utopian life, I once heard a son say to his mother:

"When will I hear the bastards cry,
Mama, when will the carrion sing?
Where are the deserts beneath the parched skies,
When will my death knell ring?
Where is the wind that howls through the ruins
Of graveyards and nations forgotten?
Why is there no lamenting and wailing
Of the painfully lost and downtrodden?
Mama, show me the men whom history claim
Did mass-murder in peacetime and war.
Show me the signs of gargantuan conflict,
Show me disease at my door.
Where is the rain that burns right through nature?
Show me her sores and her scars.
Where is the hurt and the pain between lovers?
Isn't their world much better than ours?"

VIEWPOINT.

We tend to forget in everyday life
There are other things than stress and strife.
A wide-open trail, the earth at your feet,
Humming a tune, greeting people you meet.
Smells of wood fires, cooking a meal –
The wind changes direction, the smoke makes you reel!
As the day dims, the sun does his best
Trying to set perfectly way in the West.
The stars then come out, all shimmering lights.
The girls are in town, the men are in fights.
But if you listen without any noise,
You may hear the sound of Herne out with his boys.
But if through the night, nothing you feel,
Then take that for granted – that peace is for real.
And as you go back to your daily routine,
Remember the sights and sounds you have seen.

WILL YOU?

Will you laugh if I ask you on the day of my birth
To share in the joke of my being?
Will you laugh if I ask you all through my life
For the mistakes I make in trying?

Will you sing if I ask you in the face of death
To pay my fare away?
Will you sing if I ask you at my graveside
To wing me on my way?

Will you dance if I ask you at the gates of Heaven
To get me a reprieve?
Will you dance if I ask you at the doors of Hell
To get me in with ease?

Will you mourn if I ask you after I'm gone
So I can laugh at last?
Shall we party together then, until dawn
So I can relive my past?

SHADOW SOUL.

A deathly echo resounded hollow
Within shattered shell-like walls.
A conveyance of the moody blue
Portray intricate spiraled emotion.
Static deathly hush rebounded,
Blocking relevant genius strains.
Visions hampered by tar-like night;
Severing senses, rendering useless
The mind, the body, the person within.
Taps upon exposed shoulders,
By three score six, undisguised.
Raging battles in the darkness
As instinct tries to come alive.
Blurring images whirl within
Conscious mental childlike blocks.
Instinct wins a bloody skirmish –
A leap towards the paths unknown.
Moody blue turns angry red,
Understanding again is thwarted.
Spirals begin a downward trend
As instinct waits to try again.

FRIENDSHIP.

I look upon those around me
As friends for all my years.
Those who'll see the fun in life
And those who'll stem my tears.

These certain friends I'm thinking of
Will always be around.
It's them I'll watch, it's them I'll help
And thus, I'll understand.

This understanding won't be easy,
We all know this, I think.
But as we go our daily ways,
I'll help the ones who sink.

This group of friends will all be there,
For they are dear to me.
But if we go our separate ways,
You'll all still stay with me.

Because, my friends, I'm here to say
You're all unique you'll find.
The times that you've befriended me
Are always in my mind.

UNICORN.

As I reach down through timeless eons
I regard, with pride, my descendants true.
Even though they are just part of the whole
And became enmeshed in humanities core.
Men sang their praises of fortitude and strength –
They realise their present through past heroics.
-Without my sons and daughters, men are naught.

I walked the earth when the gods were young
I seldom come where freely I roamed;
To the fathomless depths of humanity's barbarism.
Man took my kin to fight for survival:
Wrapped them up in leather bonds, and
Waged their wars with my children, their vassals.
-Without my sons and daughters, men are naught.

Down the ages the relationship changed,
The men imagined themselves the victors
And gradually raped my kin of their heritage.
We never forgot, but in time forgave
Humanity for its childlike conscience
It's still too fresh, I cannot forget.
-Without my sons and daughters, men are naught.

As I look down, my descendants flourish
Wrapped in chains their history forged.
Men are their jailers, their keepers, their captors
Not allowing them freedom. My children
With the wind in your hair and the earth at your feet,
Don't you know that you're free, until time ends?
-Without my sons and daughters, men are naught.

I relax my grip of present understanding
Tears burn my eyes and my vision blurs.
My sons and daughters have chosen their path
Though it pains me to see them so shackled and broken.
I am the thing to which they aspire,
But I cannot forget, as they have forgiven.
-Without my sons and daughters, men are naught.

VICTIM.

The floor danced with the steps of a thousand feet
Skipping in joy and mirth.
She glanced across an ill-lit room
With eyes full of promise –
But not for tonight.

As the crowd danced to the songs of their country
And the music got louder
She transfixed the eyes of her 'victim'
With a promise of tomorrow –
But not of tonight.

When the evening closed and the music ran dry,
The dancing crowd departed.
Contact was broken with pulled apart stares
He began to breathe again –
Until tomorrow.

HOPELESSNESS.

One ill thought was all it took to find
Broken hearts and silent tears.
Watching through a sunlit window
As dreams ran out to lamenting cries.

Even though the eye of jealously
Watching with apparent glee
Saw ruptured dreams rise high above
The silent dawn of understanding.

Now pain and loss were churned around
As ships on oceans, tossed and torn.
He could only see great confusion
From the reflected windows to her soul.

Time and thought will mend both their
Broken hearts and shattered dreams.
Even though she's with another
The thoughts of her he holds within.

And if the sands of time allow
Two souls to gather once again,
The songs of love and peace unending
Will give the gods their joyous hymn.

ANGER.

The anger you feel when backed in a corner
May be irrational, though for a reason.
The hurt that's been caused, violated yourself
Will be all consuming when it comes up and out.

The rages, the turmoil have found their way in,
The fort of your mind has been razed to the ground.
The wish to hit out, mental and physical
Is the path of the fallen, the damned and the sly.

So, listen my son, and heed what I tell you
The way forward in anger is not what it seems:
The only way on is to laugh from the soul,
Floating high up above the anger within.

EVERY MAN.

Every man is an island
They told me in my youth.
Every man is an island
And I took it for a truth.
Every man is an island
And I went on to believe;
As the days at school continued,
New views were not conceived.
Now out in the world I began
And I carried on believing
Every man is an island,
But it always left me grieving.
"Shit happens" as the saying goes
Seemed to happen to me.
Every man is an island,
I could no longer believe.
I have a new philosophy
And it seems to fit, I hear
"I'll do it for love or honour,
Or just a pint of beer".

CAGE.

In times that come and then may not, and life's a dream that's lost;
Reality's a figment of some other beings thought.
Our bodies are a vessel from which the soul may leave,
And feelings just a segment of all the webs we weave.
The spider is the spinner of all our paths of fate,
Our footsteps will not falter until it's all too late.
The paths compel to follow, but are they what they seem?
Is this cold hard reality, or is it but a dream?
Our feelings, love and fear, at least we'll not forsake –
Or are they just a sign of someone's give and take?
Our heart and soul are naked for one and all to see.
All life's on show, amusements, a caged menagerie.
Our show we'll keep performing: our love, our hate, our rage;
But sooner, more than later, someone must clean the cage.

THE HERMIT.

Within eternal misty spheres
A humble hermit stands alone.
Crossroads blossom, the infinite –
A spinning wheel without a name.

A former shadow of the truth,
Betwixt the past and future realms.
Dreams and choices echo hollow,
for each is piped a different tune.

Ghosts of a hundred indiscretions
Throw insubstantial chains of fear
To thwart an honest freeborn choice
And drag him to the shells below.

And through all the pillars waver
Through tears from him for those before.
Wandering outcasts, now forgotten,
To roam their paths and ne'er come home,

A glimpse of suns – fiery yellow
And there a hint of barren rocks.
He strains to see a single vision
Of summer fields in flowers clothed.

Now the testing time approaches
The choice cannot be made so soon.
He feels the rising tide of panic
Try to drown with waves of doom.

And lo a helping hand unbidden
Filled with warmth and love, unbound;
Clears his mind and warms his heart,
Now he knows he's not alone.

He takes a look at figures foreign
To gauge his worth against his dream.
He turns his back on one not worthy
And follows answers down the road.

So soon the journey nears completion.
Eyes helped him decide alone.
No matter what the guise or promise
Eyes are the window to the soul.

RITE OF PASSAGE.

She saw the fire of dancing smoke
Calling from a distant hilltop.
The call replied by flames aloft,
A message for them not to stop.

As she watched the smoke grew thick,
Dancing figures seen within.
Wraiths and shadows danced with death,
The rite of passage to begin.

She watched the boy arrive, alone.
In purest gold and dressed in skins.
Reflecting light of flames without,
Matching to the fire within.

Men appeared with faces stern
And called the boy towards the flames.
She heard their voices raised in song,
The words lost in space and time.

She waited there with bated breath.
Above, the sound of drums.
The screams and shouts of pending joy,
The rite of passage nearly done.

The boy emerged, now a man,
Through flames, and fire, and friends.
The woman laughed; her son had passed.
The rite of passage at an end.

SHATTERED.

Shattered memories, shattered thoughts,
Entombed in shattered glass.
Crystal fragments appear to me
As bits of shattered past.

Cracked reflections all around
Stare from eye to I;
Portraying things I'd soon forget
Which will cling until I die.

The blasting furnace has cooled off
And left a cairn of waste.
These bits and bobs by which I'll forge
The life on which I'm based.

BEGINNINGS.

Walking my way as I normally do,
My eyes just three feet in front,
I tend to miss the natural joys
Of a nature.

The one time I do look ahead,
A radiant flower I see.
It shines, it glows, and I hear it say
"Look at me".

I stop and stare and all the time,
This beauty is there before me.
My eyes glaze over, my mind goes bright:
It's perfect!

Happily, would I just stand and stay
With this bright jewel in mind.
But I must go on, though before I do
I say "speak".

It turns itself, this flower of beauty,
Its eyes look right through my soul.
The words of meaning are perfectly clear:
"Can you see?"

At last my eyes are opening up
I take the time to look out,
Towards the beauty that's all around.
It's a start.

REINCARNATION.

And though my soul still cries to see
The memories of lives.
The ones I've lived, the ones I've lost;
Through which my soul survived.

In one I know I was a hound,
My master most I loved.
But for him my life was shed,
Through wounds and pouring blood.

I came again dressed as a man,
A conqueror, no less.
Pulled down the country of my roots
And I did call it just.

In this the life which I now live,
I strive to understand
The wonders which I learn and breathe –
It's those I'll leave for man.

And I do know I'll come again,
The guise I can't foresee.
But I can only hope and pray,
My knowledge stays with me.

THE WHEEL.

People live, people laugh,
They love and they cry;
But why on earth
Are they afraid to die?

To have such emotion
So fettered and bound
'tis not of nature,
But tied to the ground.

Through a process that's learned,
To change what is real;
The path is now clear,
To be free from the wheel.

<u>DREAMS.</u>

Within a dream I'll dream a dream
Of a time within the summer lands.
Where gentle folk do dwell within
In timeless, ageless, measured spans.

Within this dream, I'll dream a dream
Of grass and trees and flowers
And through them dancing merrily
Are folk enthroned in colour.

I'll dream the dream of time itself
And thus, be of the throng.
To seek the knowledge, I have sought
That man has since forgotten.

We'll dream the dream of knowledge now,
It is for this I have striven.
For knowledge be it freely taught,
So be it freely given.

THE LADY.

I saw a lady upon a hill
Stood as still as stone.
Her hair was spun as webs of gold,
Her eyes as precious stones.

She raised her hand and beckoned me;
Her smile, it shone so true.
Her gaze flowed through me to the bone,
Her voice like summer's dew.

She spoke in words I understood,
Though the language was unlearned;
Her words were warm and comforting,
Once done, she smiled and turned.

And so, do I now follow her
To wonders I'd not seen.
Of love, of joy, of friends, of birth,
Of things I'd never dreamed.

The lady is around me still,
Just slightly out of reach.
Watching me absorb and learn,
But always there to teach.

The lady now to me is known,
Goddess is she to some.
To me she is both mother, friend,
And sister, all in one.

FIGURE IN GREY.

On the darkest of nights
With an absence of light
It came to steal a soul.

"Where did it come from?"

It came from far away
Amidst shadows of grey
Unknown, unheard, unsung.

"Who did it come for?"

Child, that's a long song
My time is now done
It is not the place to tell.

"but I must know!"

Then listen:

Not much is known about the figure in grey
Cloaked in colours of no description;
Away in the land of the midnight sun,
A superstition, or so they say.

Not much is known about this figure in grey,
A wanderer in the dreams of strangers.
Giving a gift of knowledge and foresight
To those who seek a balanced way.

He came to me, this figure in grey
In a field within the northern isle.
His cloak a rainbow in the sight of dream eyes,
A vision of truth to begin my day.

As I succumbed to the shock and reality
A new thing shown by this figure in grey.
Visions of peace, of beauty, possibilities –
A silver radiance of fatal serenity.

And while I dwelt in the peace and the harmony
Of that foggy, windswept northern isle.
The ancient wonderous gardens of Babylon
Couldn't compare to the beauty around me.

He turned to go, this figure in grey
I called him to stay for a while.
At this he stopped, removed his cloak.
It was me I saw reflected in grey.

I have seen the grey wanderer
I have seen him in my dreams,
I have seen him in my nightmares,
And he held me while I screamed.

WANDERER.

A wanderer I shall now be
To walk my path of truth,
And there shall find, in hills un-roamed,
The dreams as yet unread.

But in these dreams, though undefined,
The dice of fortune's cast;
Wherein the grace of Father Time,
Shall light my winding path.

For only he can have the say
As to when my time is done.
With light and key, he can but mark
My path from start to end.

For he was there before my birth
And shall remain long after.
And if someone reads the words I leave,
They may gain that one step further.

MEMORIES.

I clothe myself in shrouds of mist
Cocooned within remembered spheres,
And underneath the full moon's light,
I witness words, to face a fear.

Lo, open sight, the sheltered eyes
With clear intent but mischievous gaze.
I can no longer see direct,
But remember glances, through misty haze.

Feelings of an intense worth
Flash through the mist and score
Against my soul another scar,
To list with those that went before.

The mist itself is paradox –
Continues on and standing still.
Resounding echoes, hollow din,
In places where the heart once filled.

To dream a dream, and dream again
Of fantasy, of hope, of fact.
The moon is dim, diminished by
The light of day, 'til night comes back.

ACKNOWLEDGEMENTS

It is with profound gratitude that I wish to thank all those who have encouraged me to get these poems into print (Ok it has taken me years, so thanks again for your persistence and patience!)

Thanks, must also go to my family for continuously being there in support and encouragement. Especially to the late Sheila Porter, my grandmother, for her unique view on life and all those late-night conversations about life, the universe and everything – it's those conversations that started my writing.

Thanks also to Ale Ramirez for helping me reconnect with who I am, and to my extended family at Your Growth Game, for the support and encouragement in this and many other areas of my life.

Thanks also to Andy Harrington and everyone at the PSA – your encouragement and guidance are a constant inspiration.

A more than honorable mention must go to the Universe, God, Higher self (however you see it) for the continuous reminders that I am human, fallible but full of potential. It is only through understanding this, that I continue to grow and develop myself in ways that I never thought possible. For this I am eternally grateful.

Finally, but by no means least, thanks to you for reading this work. It is my hope that you can see relevance and insight in the words I have written and that it helps you on your own journey, wherever it may take you.

Remember, you are a child of the Universe, a child of the stars, born to shine and stand out. You deserve to live the life of your dreams and to achieve the heights of your ambition. You are on a life-journey that will take you anywhere and everywhere, but, occasionally, stop and take a breath, and have real gratitude for how far you have already come.

Charlie

ABOUT THE AUTHOR

Charlie is passionate about helping people overcome their fear and for them to live that life they only thought of as a dream.

He is an award winning international public speaker, life and motivation coach who firmly believes in everyone's ability to live without fear, to change their mindset and to achieve the goals and ambitions they set for themselves – no matter what they are.

Having spent over 20 years working in the Private Security Sector both in the U.K. and abroad, he has had to face his own fears and demons on a regular basis and has, through his own experience, found ways to deal with and overcome fear when it arises.

Charlie now works at Happiness Inc and splits his time between helping individuals realise what fears are holding them back from achieving their goals; and working with companies to create inclusive and beneficial working practices to reduce fear and stress in the workplace.

Any spare time he has will find him roaming the countryside with his trusty sidekick, River – a 9yo Husky X rescue.

For more information visit:

www.happinessinc.life

www.facebook.com/livehappinessinc

www.instagram.com/happyincpics

www.linkedin.com/in/charlie-hirst-

www.ingramcontent.com/pod-product-compliance
Lightning Source LLC
LaVergne TN
LVHW020528160826
845677LV00015B/3960